ALTO SAX

HIGH SCHOOL MUSICAL

D1105436

HOW TO USE THE CD ACCOMPANIMENT:

A MELODY CUE APPEARS ON THE RIGHT CHANNEL ONLY. IF YOUR CD PLAYER HAS A BALANCE ADJUSTMENT, YOU CAN ADJUST THE VOLUME OF THE MELODY BY TURNING DOWN THE RIGHT CHANNEL.

ISBN 1-4234-1285-0

Disney characters and artwork © Disney Enterprises, Inc.

Walt Disney Music Company

DISTRIBUTED BY

HAL•LEONARD®
CORPORATION

7777 W. BLUEMOUND RD. P.O. BOX 13819 MILWAUKEE, WI 53213

Visit Hal Leonard Online at
www.halleonard.com

BOP TO THE TOP

ALTO SAX

Words and Music by RANDY PETERSEN
and KEVIN QUINN

2 BREAKING FREE

ALTO SAX

Words and Music by
JAMIE HOUSTON

❸ GET'CHA HEAD IN THE GAME

ALTO SAX

Words and Music by RAY CHAM,
GREG CHAM and ANDREW SEELEY

(Spoken:) Get - 'cha, get - 'cha, get - 'cha, get - 'cha head in the game. _ Whoo! ___

◆4 I CAN'T TAKE MY EYES OFF OF YOU

ALTO SAX

Words and Music by MATTHEW GERRARD
and ROBBIE NEVIL

START OF SOMETHING NEW

ALTO SAX

Words and Music by MATTHEW GERRARD
and ROBBIE NEVIL

D.S. al Coda

CODA

◆6 STICK TO THE STATUS QUO

ALTO SAX

Words and Music by DAVID N. LAWRENCE
and FAYE GREENBERG

7 WE'RE ALL IN THIS TOGETHER

ALTO SAX

Words and Music by MATTHEW GERRARD
and ROBBIE NEVIL

⬧8 WHAT I'VE BEEN LOOKING FOR

ALTO SAX

Words and Music by ANDY DODD
and ADAM WATTS

◆ 9 WHEN THERE WAS ME AND YOU

ALTO SAX

Words and Music by
JAMIE HOUSTON